HOW TO
GET EVEN
WITH
YOUR BOSS

**BY
ROGER AND BARBARA SOROCHTY**

**CARTOONS BY
MARK LEWIS**

**EDITED BY
KARL P. LOWENBERG**

GOLLEHON BOOKS
GRAND RAPIDS, MI

MANUFACTURED IN THE UNITED STATES OF AMERICA

Library of Congress Catalog Card Number: 92-73346

ISBN 0-914839-29-2
(International Standard Book Number)

GOLLEHON BOOKS are published by: Gollehon Press, Inc., 6157
28th St. S.E., Grand Rapids, MI 49546. Gollehon Books are available
in quantity purchases; contact Special Sales. Gollehon does not
accept unsolicited manuscripts. Brief book proposals are reviewed.

Contents

This book is dedicated to our parents, Anna and Peter Stasiuk and Helen and Charles Sorochty, whose love and support taught us about success and survival. We also dedicate this book to Matthew and Michelle, who make us proud to be their parents and who have a knack for keeping everything in perspective.

INTRODUCTION

The working world is increasingly punctuated by the inescapable reality of stress. It must be endured but no one ever said that you couldn't face it without a good sense of humor. The predominance of two-career families can be singled out as a major contributor to these stressful situations especially as one spouse or the other deals with the ups and downs of building a career. The challenge is in balancing career, family, and individual needs. All of these factors can take a toll on even the most solid of relationships.

As a two-career family, we experienced many moves to ensure advancement in our chosen fields. We often found these transitions to be stressful and that the best release for tension and stress during these volatile times was tied to humor. Day-to-day events which sometimes seemed cataclysmic became manageable when we laughed together.

Perhaps the most important person who can either minimize or increase the level of stress one feels at work is. . . THE BOSS. Every working person has one and they come in a variety of personalities, management styles, and emotional and psychological stabilities.

Where the boss is a factor in the stress you feel at work, one's natural reaction may be to become conciliatory and defensive in order to protect one's job. Away from the workplace, however, one can easily take the offensive by fantasizing about how you might really respond to the boss — by getting even.

On the premise that a touch of humor and lightheartedness make even the most stressful situations bearable — we have written this book to offer a chuckle and the encouragement to rise in the morning and face yet another day at work. We offer these fantasies only for the humor we hope they will provide during difficult and stressful times in your work life. We don't recommend you do any of these things. Just thinking about the deeds can break the tension and place things in perspective. Just imagining the dastardly deed can be ever so much more satisfying.

We hope these pages bring a laugh in the middle of a particularly difficult work day or just make you feel better. Good luck! Hang in there, and remember no matter how stressful or bleak things look, better days are ahead.

Roger and Barbara Sorochty

CHAPTER 1

Annoying
The
Boss

2 ANNOYING THE BOSS

While the boss is on vacation have the boss's car painted purple and "Born to Boogie" painted in bright yellow across the side.

Place the boss's name and business address on a pornographic mailing list.

Have the lock changed on the boss's office door.

Let the air out of two of the boss's tires (one front and one rear, of course).

Let 101 Gophers loose in the boss's yard.

Substitute glue stick material for the boss's lip balm.

Have the boss's home telephone number changed. . . and unlisted.

Send the boss a get well card. . . when there's no sign of illness.

Make one of the legs on the boss's desk and chair shorter than the others.

Have the boss's office moved to the basement of the building.

Remove the blades on the boss's electric lawn mower.

Advertise an estate auction at the boss's home the same day the boss has planned to have a big party there.

If your boss is a he, have the tailor pick up his suits while he's out of town with a request that the slacks be shortened two inches.

Send a change of address notification to the post office for your boss's home address.

Rig the boss's doorbell so it plays "It's A Small World" every time it is pushed.

Enter the boss in a nude bungee-jumping contest.

Have the boss's car filled with fast-drying cement.

◆

Have all of the boss's undergarments starched.

◆

Late at night spray plant killer on the boss's flower beds.

◆

Send the boss flowers with poison ivy serving as the greenery.

◆

Have the neighborhood's newspapers delivered to the boss's home stating that the neighbors are on vacation and the boss is collecting the newspapers.

Leave a message on the boss's answering machine that says: "This is very important. . . a matter of life and death. . ." Don't finish the message.

Call ten real estate agents and tell them that you want to sell your (the boss's) house. Arrange to have them come to the boss's home on ten consecutive nights.

Have all of the locks changed on the boss's house.

Fill the boss's office with beer cans. . . ceiling to floor and wall to wall.

Place ground poison ivy leaves in his jock-itch powder.

Have three pigs delivered to the boss's home.

Send the boss a letter from the bank saying they were informed that the boss's property taxes have increased 300%.

Call the boss's insurance company and tell them to cancel the automobile insurance because you (the boss) have decided to go with another company.

Place 50 "For Sale By Owner" signs in the boss's front yard.

Erase all the boss's cassette tapes and replace with Lawrence Welk's greatest hits.

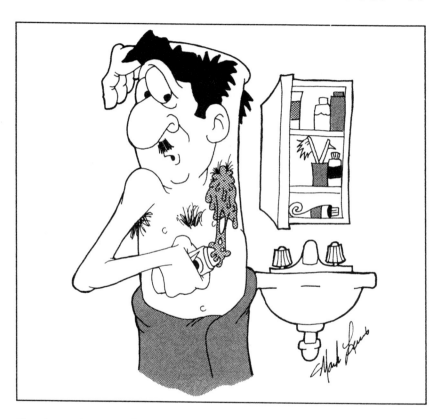

Replace the boss's roll-on deodorant with rubber cement.

When the boss gets on the elevator, arrange for it to get stuck between floors and make sure the elevator is filled with unsavory characters.

When you are invited to the boss's house for a party, bring a matchbox filled with mating cockroaches and let them out in the kitchen.

Put head lice inside the boss's favorite golf cap.

Substitute the boss's petroleum jelly with hemorrhoid shrinking medicine.

Cancel the boss's health insurance.

Replace the fluid in your boss's nasal spray bottle with extract of cayenne pepper.

Place nuts and bolts inside the boss's tires so anytime the car runs it sounds like it's going to fall apart.

Arrange to have the entire office speak in pig latin and act as if the boss has lost his ability to comprehend language.

Have the entire office come to work in animal costumes and act like they are dressed normally.

Replace the boss's maple syrup with syrup of Ipecac to induce vomiting.

Glue everything down on the boss's desk.

Have the boss's treadmill adjusted so it automatically moves from slow to super fast in seconds.

Put super glue in the boss's Grecian Formula.

Place an ad in the newspaper announcing a sure-fire way to get rich. Use your boss's phone number at home as the contact.

Have four feet of artificial snow trucked to and piled around the boss's house.

Put some scratches on the boss's prized CD's.

Have the boss's office furniture glued to the ceiling in the position where it should appear on the floor.

Drill holes the size of pinholes in the boss's pots and pans.

Pay someone who hasn't bathed in a while to sit right next to the boss in a movie theatre. When the boss moves, have the unwelcomed neighbor follow the boss to the new seat.

Replace the boss's after-shave with paint remover.

Have a Volkswagen assembled in the boss's office.

✦

Refill the boss's eye-wash bottle with onion juice.

✦

Cancel the boss's life insurance.

✦

Send the boss a truckload of coal for Christmas.

✦

Replace the fish in the boss's tropical fish tank with fish skeletons.

Put tabasco sauce in the boss's morning coffee.

Replace the boss's shampoo with Nair... presto... no hair.

Wait until the boss leaves for vacation then get a container of Limburger cheese and leave it opened on the counter until the boss returns.

Weld the driver's seat in the boss's car in the position closest to the steering wheel.

◆

Run a notice in the paper that announces the establishment of a temporary home for the homeless at the boss's home address.

Put a plastic human skeleton in the boss's swimming pool after it's been covered for winter.

Have a sound device installed in the boss's office that consistently emits an annoying droning sound that you shut off the minute the boss asks any guests if the droning sound is annoying them. When they leave you start the noise again.

Let grubs loose in the boss's yard.

Put ink in the boss's windshield wiper solution.

When the boss arrives at that special vacation spot have a telegram waiting asking the boss to return to the office for an important meeting that could make or break the business.

Have the boss's tennis racket strings loosened.

Sew velcro on the boss's slacks and a velcro strip to the office chair the boss sits on.

Send the boss an expensive Scotch or other favorite drink and make sure it is watered down.

Have a sign put on the boss's lawn that says, "Sales People Welcomed."

Replace the boss's toothpaste with Preparation H.

Change all the street signs around in the boss's neighborhood the night of his big "thank you" party for customers.

Have a helicopter hover over the boss's house at 3 a.m. with someone on a bullhorn asking the occupants to come out with their hands raised.

◆

Have all the clocks in the office set 10 minutes ahead of time.

Spray weed killer or bleach on the boss's lawn spelling out the message, "My spouse beats me twice a day whether I need it or not."

When the office orders out for lunch make sure the boss's lunch gets a hefty dose of hot sauce.

Substitute the boss's luggage for the big business trip overseas with luggage packed for the opposite sex.

Rig the boss's chair so you can give the boss a slight shock at will.

Have the main electrical circuit breaker in the boss's home go out every night at 9 p.m.

✦

File bankruptcy in the boss's name.

✦

Invite the boss's son's fraternity brothers (all 102) home for spring break.

✦

Inform the boss that a multi-millionaire who is interested in sealing a lucrative business deal is arriving by private jet at the airport and expects the boss to pick him and his party up at 2:30 a.m.

Have two inches sawed off the boss's boardroom chair only.

Put itching powder in the boss's body talc.

Replace fertilized eggs for the usual eggs in the boss's refrigerator.

Have an estate sale scheduled at the boss's home on the day he returns from vacation.

Replace the liquor in the boss's liquor cabinet with colored water.

Send a letter informing the boss that the company wants him to take early retirement.

Fabricate huge orders with erroneous part numbers that are to be shipped to actual customers COD as per the boss's orders.

◆

Let some garter snakes loose in the boss's house.

◆

Introduce a virus into your boss's personal computer.

◆

Send all employees a letter from the boss announcing the first-ever profit-sharing plan in the company's history.

Tell the boss the employees are having a drawing for a turkey. The boss's name is the only name on all the entries. When the boss wins, have a 35-pound live, mean turkey delivered and chained to the boss's desk.

Make up a special batch of treats for the boss. Leave them on the boss's desk before work begins in honor of boss's day. The treat is dog-food nibbles rolled in powdered sugar.

Have a barbed-wire fence without a gate erected around the boss's house overnight.

Fill the boss's hair spray atomizer with green paint.

Have the boss's radio headsets for jogging permanently set on a "heavy-metal" station.

Send your boss a letter on corporate station-ery that states, "Due to an effort to right-size the company, your position has been eliminated."

Have your boss's medical records transfer-red to a veterinarian.

Before the boss's next business trip send notification from the travel agent that the airline has recalled most of its planes but not to worry, they think the defect has been fixed.

Put a smoke bomb in the boss's desk.

For that all-important awards dinner, have the boss's tux returned to him from the cleaners but in place of the traditional style, have a gold lamé suit substituted with no chance that the original can be delivered in time.

✦

Smear shaving cream on all the windows of the boss's home.

✦

Check the boss's luggage in at the airport with it tagged to Vladivostok, Siberia.

✦

Send the boss a box of dead queen bees disguised as chocolates.

Have all the locks to the keys that the boss owns changed.

✦

Dump 16 cartons of Jello into the boss's swimming pool.

✦

Leave word at the office that the President of the United States needs to speak to the boss as soon as possible.

✦

Put cat litter on the boss's porch while the boss is on vacation.

✦

Train 2,500 homing pigeons to return to the boss's home and roost on the roof.

Place a snake in the boss's toilet.

When the boss is out of town, have all the switches in the boss's home rewired to activate the garage door.

◆

Disconnect the starter in the boss's car.

◆

Take your boss's eyeglasses to a one-hour eyeglass store and have the prescription changed... just a little... every week.

◆

Announce that the boss is supporting a "Buy American" campaign and will donate a $1,000 bonus to every employee buying an American-made car.

Arrange to have the boss's prized AKC breeding dog neutered.

♦

Remove all the boss's suits from the closet and replace them with fast-food restaurant uniforms.

♦

Bend the shafts on the boss's golf clubs just enough to throw off his game.

♦

Have the boss's shoes bronzed.

♦

Replace the sugar in the boss's sugar bowl with alum.

Find the boss's top administrative assistant a better-paying job with the competition.

If your boss carries a beeper, beep your boss at inappropriate times and leave the number of the local strip joint.

Replace your boss's shoes with identical pairs; some of which are a half size smaller and others which are a half size larger.

Have a sign placed on the boss's lawn that announces dogs and their owners are welcomed for "relief."

Pay off a waiter at a plush restaurant the boss frequents to dump his dinner in his lap.

Have the lights in the boss's office gradually dim so the boss will think the eyesight is the first thing to go.

Have 20 pounds of fish delivered in the heat of summer to the boss's home. Make sure everyone will be gone for the day.

Put a ball bearing under the insole of one of the boss's shoes.

Slip steroids in the boss's coffee every day for 6 months.

CHAPTER 2

Getting The Boss In Trouble

Send the boss a fictitious letter from a Fortune 500 company indicating the boss's election as chairman of the board and inviting the boss to the next stockholders meeting.

If your boss is a he, let his wife know by letter that you plan to file a paternity suit against him. If your boss is a she, send a letter to her husband announcing that the child she put up for adoption is looking for her.

Have 60 Hell's Angels show up at the boss's house for a party.

Place a bumper sticker on the boss's car that says, "I hate cops."

Have the boss's credit cards cancelled just before an important business trip.

Send love letters to the boss's home.

Send the boss's resume out for other positions. . . preferably in foreign countries.

Send a letter notifying the boss that the IRS will conduct an audit of the boss's taxes for the last seven years.

Arrange for the boss's home to be painted purple while the boss is on vacation.

Send a box of laxatives to the boss disguised as candy.

Send the boss's letter of resignation to the chairman of the board.

Have an escort service arrive to pick up the boss's spouse for a night on the town.

Place a position announcement for the boss's job with the local newspaper.

Substitute the boss's wife's birth-control pills with placebos.

Enroll the boss in a Biker's Club.

Send the boss notification that his home failed a termite inspection.

Have a professional wrestler show up at the boss's home carrying a note that the boss supposedly authored calling the wrestler a lily-livered wimp.

Issue an ultimatum to the board from the boss stating, "Double my salary or take this job and shove it."

Fill the boss's fountain pen with disappearing ink.

Send a letter from the boss's former spouse declaring that the divorce was never finalized.

Invite the boss's mother-in-law for a two-month visit.

Have fast-multiplying piranah dumped into the boss's swimming pool.

Have a bullseye sewn on the boss's jacket.

Send a note to the IRS indicating that, as the boss's former accountant, you know that the boss lied about information on tax returns for the last ten years.

Review your workplace for any safety or health violations and report them anonymously as a concerned citizen.

Send the boss's spouse a sympathy card expressing sorrow for being married to the SOB.

Send a memo in the boss's name to all management staff announcing an emergency staff meeting on Sunday morning.

◆

Set all of the boss's clocks back by 20 minutes.

◆

Arrange for an escort service to arrive at the boss's home when the boss's spouse is there.

◆

Let the FBI know that your boss has made threats on the president's life.

Send to the editorial page of the local paper long, rambling letters, making no sense, in your boss's name.

If your boss is a he, leave a bra and panties in the glove compartment of the family car. If the boss is a she, leave boxer shorts and a T-shirt.

Inform former candidates for a position with the company that the reason they weren't hired by the boss was because they were too ugly.

Send a year's subscription to Playboy to the boss's minister with the boss's compliments.

Put limburger cheese in the boss's deodorant stick.

Plant marijuana seeds in the boss's garden; wait 3 months and then call the cops.

Install a silent security system in the boss's home when the boss is away. The boss will get arrested breaking and entering upon returning home.

Tell the boss the president of the multi-million dollar company with whom he is negotiating the deal of a lifetime is hard of hearing and the boss should yell during the negotiations.

Loosen the bindings on the boss's skis.

Check out everything on the boss's resume. If errors are found be sure that appropriate people (like board members and the media) know.

Send an invitation in the boss's name to the city's top twenty-five executives and spouses announcing an exclusive party at one of the city's best restaurants. Naturally, there will be no party.

Put a laxative in the boss's coffee two hours before an important presentation.

Send flowers and candy to the boss's home with a card that says, "Thanks for a wonderful evening, darling."

✦

Have an actress costumed as a bride arrive at the boss's home for their wedding.

✦

Send a letter from the boss to the in-laws inviting them to move in with the boss's family.

✦

Send the boss's spouse a blank check for shopping at an exclusive local department store.

Put the boss's name and address on every magazine subscription post card you can find.

Place a tape player in the boss's trunk that repeats at five-minute intervals: "I'm locked in the trunk and I can't get out."

Turn 30 cats loose at the boss's house then call the ASPCA and report the boss for harboring an excessive number of pets.

Change the boss's budget submissions so headquarters questions the boss's capabilities.

While the boss's spouse is away, have divorce papers served.

Send a letter to the boss's office incriminating the boss in an embezzlement plot.

Hire an actress to play the daughter the boss never knew existed from that affair... a long time ago. She should call on her long-lost parent at an appropriate time at the office.

List the boss's home in the real-estate section of the newspaper as being "for sale by owner."

Cancel the boss's wife's credit cards.

Send the production line layoff notices two hours before an important order is scheduled to be filled.

✦

Send a memo in the boss's name to all management staff giving them the following Monday off.

✦

Send flowerless roses (thorny stems only) to the boss's mother-in-law for her birthday.

✦

Submit the boss's picture and biographical data (greatly enhanced) to a video-dating firm.

Send a telegram to a reputed gangster indicating that the boss has been seen in compromising situations with the mobster's spouse.

Send love letters from the boss to the most happily married person of the opposite sex in the office.

◆

Send a letter to the State Department indicating that the boss is involved in espionage.

◆

Tell the boss's child that there is no Santa Claus, the Tooth Fairy uses pliers, and the Easter Bunny is dead.

CHAPTER 3

Embarrassing
The Boss

For the boss's next birthday, send a care package that contains everything the boss will need to navigate old age: hemorrhoid cream, denture cream, bi-focals, bran cereal, wrinkle creams, etc.

◆

Have a Mass or religious ceremony dedicated to your boss's memory at your boss's church.

◆

Tell the boss a notice arrived saying that the boss flunked the company's stress test.

◆

Pay off a barber to shave the back of the boss's head.

If your boss is a male, send a package of condoms to his home marked "Extra Small."

Inform the boss that the client arriving for dinner has a very weak stomach and the best meal to serve is farina with milk, tapioca pudding, and plain yogurt.

Send the boss a telegram saying that a long-lost relative will be arriving that evening. At the appropriate time have a chimpanzee delivered to the boss's home.

Have an undertaker dispatched to pick up the boss's body at the office.

◆

Send a notice with the boss's signature to all employees indicating that the company will increase the retirement benefits by 20%.

Sew catnip into the lining of the boss's coat.

Sit across from the boss at an important meeting, chew tobacco, and spit into a beer can.

Invite all employees to a big bash at the boss's home. The invitation states that only a few selected staff members were invited so it's to be kept top secret. Will the boss be surprised when the door bell rings... and rings... and rings.

When the boss is scheduled to give a slide presentation, substitute the slide tray with one holding slides of the mating habits of the Trobriand Islanders.

Offer lodging at the boss's home to a homeless family.

◆

Invite the boss to an exclusive party to which the boss wasn't invited.

◆

Send the boss notification that all of the boss's credit cards have been cancelled.

◆

Send a telegram saying that the boss has been selected Citizen of the Year for your city. The next day send another telegram saying that there had been a mistake and that a noted community leader (someone the boss views as a competitor) will receive the award.

In a letter from the boss's personal physician, notify the boss that brain surgery is needed.

Send the boss a telegram asking the boss to appear on the Tonight Show.

Send letters to the editor in your boss's name that nominate your city as a nuclear-waste dump site.

Have horns air-brushed on the boss's formal portrait for the annual report.

Arrange a hot-air balloon ride for the boss. Let the boss get in the basket then "accidentally" let the safety lines go before the pilot gets in.

Call Alcoholics Anonymous and have information sent to the boss in care of the chairman of the board's address.

Invite the boss to go ice skating on a pond where the ice has not completely frozen.

Have the soles on the boss' shoes as well as the office floors highly polished and waxed.

Send in the clowns for the boss's formal dinner party.

Send out a press release indicating that, as a history buff, the boss most admires Adolph Hitler, Vlad the Impaler, Joseph Stalin, Manuel Noriega, and Saddam Hussein.

Invite the boss to the social event of the year. Formal wear is the order of the evening but tell the boss it's a toga party.

Every night get the boss's dictation tapes and insert embarrassing statements.

Have two bus-loads of rambunctious kindergartners dropped off at the boss's home.

Enroll the boss in charm school.

◆

Send the boss's obituary notice to the newspaper.

◆

Have the elastic on the boss's jogging shorts stretched so when he goes for a run at the club his shorts will end up around his ankles.

◆

Train pigeons to zero in on the boss's favorite pool chair. When the boss goes to sunbathe — bombs away.

Train a turkey vulture to perch over the boss's door.

Send a letter informing the boss that the bank is foreclosing on the mortgage.

Invite local dignitaries to attend a special lunch at the boss's office but be sure the boss is out of town for the event.

Send the boss a book addressing ways to overcome impotency.

Send the boss a fake letter from a publisher indicating there is a good deal of interest in writing a book about the boss's life.

Put chemicals in the boss's pool that will stain skin yellow.

Send insulting notes from the boss to the chairman of the board's spouse.

Send the boss notification from the boss's alma mater that a mistake has been made on the boss's credit hours and the boss needs two more courses to graduate.

♦

Inform the boss that you have knowledge of a special promotion a radio station is running at the local shopping mall. If the boss parades through the mall in underwear and carrying a parasol the boss will win $100,000.

Send a letter to prominent individuals with a fabricated hard-luck story about your boss and include an address where financial help, cards, and letters can be sent.

Send the boss an "I've admired you from afar" letter from Julia Roberts (Michael Douglas, as appropriate.)

Invite the boss to a formal party. Tell everyone else to dress casually.

Enroll the boss in some remedial management courses at the local university.

Arrange to have the boss kidnapped, stripped, smeared with catnip, and tied to a statue in the city park.

When the boss needs a limousine for the city's annual charity ball — order a garbage truck to pick up the boss instead.

Train a turkey vulture to fly above the boss's car every time he leaves the office.

Arrange to have the boss address a deaf organization meeting on the importance of hiring the handicapped. Then have the signer tell jokes during the boss's whole speech.

Inform the police that there is a body buried in the boss's backyard.

Place aluminum foil inside the lining of the boss's coat so when going through airport security checks, the alarms will ring, and ring, and ring.

Pay off the young child of a colleague to yell loudly, "Look, mommy, your boss has hair growing out of his ears."

Send a press release to the tabloids that states: "(The Boss) says UFO lands, takes him aboard, mates, and that he will give birth in three years."

Sew all the flies shut on the boss's slacks.

Have the boss's lunch delivered in a Roy Rogers lunch box.

Place a sticker on the boss's back before he volunteers for the homeless shelter that says, "Get a job, loser."

Slip a yellow dye tablet into the boss's swimsuit pocket before the annual company swim party.

Have a glass with false teeth placed in the executive washroom with the boss's name predominantly visible on the glass.

Have 10 "porta potties" delivered to the boss's home.

Reverse the wiring on the boss's thermostat so that it will be on high in summer and on low in winter.

Replace the boss's coffee cup with one that dribbles.

Send the boss a letter indicating his testosterone (her estrogen) level is not high enough to be inducted into the new exclusive men's (women's) club that is coming to town.

Attach mittens with clips to the boss's winter coat.

Submit an article to the tabloids with a headline that reads, "Jackass born in (boss's home town) with human head (a picture of the boss's head on the jackass).

Send the boss a cellulose bathing suit that will disintegrate when the boss hits the water.

Put a package of gum on the boss's desk that will turn teeth black when chewed.

Circulate a rumor that the boss is a member of a witches coven.

Put rubber shafts on the boss's golf clubs.

Send the boss notification that the boss has been nominated to "Who's Who in America." Then, post a letter on the bulletin board confirming that the nomination has been rejected.

Have a box of adult diapers delivered to the boss at the office.

Sit in the front row during the boss's report to stockholders and suck on a huge lemon.

Cut two holes in the seat of the boss's pants.

Inform the boss he walked in his sleep in the nude and a tabloid television show will be airing his stroll on the next installment.

Stage a murder in the secretary pool and when the boss leaves to call 911 everything returns to normal.

Have actors hold up the boss in the main office area with a sizeable audience. They make the boss strip to underwear, put on lipstick and sing "Lady of Spain."

Send a priest to do an exorcism on the night your boss attends a costume party attired as a ghoul.

Make UFO imprints on your boss's lawn and convince the boss to report the landing to the media.

Put a sleeping pill in the boss's morning coffee and when the boss dozes off, tattoo his forearm with "Born to Boogie."

Invite the boss to a non-existent White House party.

Send the boss a parrot that knows every dirty word in the book.

When your boss is entertaining a very important group of people, arrange for the waiter to tell the boss that the credit card has been rejected.

Call your boss's secretary when you know the boss is out of town and leave the following message: "Big Louie says to put the cash under the fifth trash can on Third Street around the corner from the Second Chance Saloon."

Tell everyone in the office to give the boss the raspberries on a certain day and let them know that the boss is expecting this treatment as part of a lost wager.

Place a lawn sign wishing the boss Happy Birthday but increase the boss's age by 15 years.

Learn to throw your voice so that at important meetings with the boss it appears that embarrassing body sounds are coming from the boss's direction.

Set off a rotten egg bomb under the boss's chair during an important board of directors meeting.

Post the boss's cellular phone number in every bar in town with the message: for a good time call. . .

On the day the boss is scheduled for an important business trip have the car towed for repairs and then report it stolen to the police.

Send a memo from the boss indicating that from the next day forward everyone in the office must take their shoes off and approach the copy machine on their knees.

Put sleeping pills in the boss's coffee and when he falls asleep, have a golden hoop earring pierced in his nose.

If your boss is a he, send him a telegram from a "television producer" indicating your boss will receive a $5000 check if he wears a dress to work and allows the program to videotape his arrival at the office.

Put the boss's picture on a wanted poster at the post office.

Pat the boss on the back and leave a sticker that reads, "I'm not wearing any underwear today. . . and I feel GREAT!"

Send your boss a dress-for-success analysis with suggestions that will do anything but ensure success.

Invite the boss to the local television station for an interview. When the boss arrives, no one there will know why.

CHAPTER 4

Spending The Boss's Money

Call the boss's alma mater and make a $10,000 pledge in the boss's name.

Send an invitation to an exclusive party to the city's top 25 executives and their spouses inviting them to the city's most exclusive restaurant. Tell the maitre'd to send the bill to the boss.

Select an exclusive mail-order catalog and charge $10,000 to the boss's American Express card.

◆

Call the garage and tell them that the boss's car won't start and have it towed in for repairs.

Order $500 worth of Girl Scout cookies in the boss's name.

Order six custom silk shirts (or blouses) in the boss's name. . . with the neck size one-half inch too small.

Get the boss's credit card number and purchase two non-refundable tickets to Paris on the Concorde.

While the boss is on vacation, call a landscaper and have the boss's yard totally redone as a natural prairie.

Send the boss a telegram saying that the boss has won the Publishers' Clearinghouse Sweepstakes with instructions to fly to Peoria, Illinois to claim the prize.

Call the boss's spouse and tell her to pick him up at the local topless bar.

Have flowers delivered to the boss's spouse with the correct last name but the wrong first name.

Send a note from the church thanking the boss for donating 20% of the boss's salary as a yearly donation.

Have fast-multiplying algae dumped into the boss's pool.

While the boss is on vacation, have the driveway taken out... but don't have it replaced.

Have a Mercedes shipped to the boss's home direct from Germany... along with the bill.

Announce the establishment of a scholarship in the boss's name to the local university.

Reserve season tickets with all the local sports franchises and charge them to the boss.

Turn 5 pounds of termites loose on your boss's prized mohogany sailboat.

Order one of everything from the Home Shopping Network and charge the items to the boss's account.

Have ten suits specially designed by a leading fashion designer delivered to the boss's home along with the bill.

Send a letter stating that the boss's home has unusually high levels of radon gas and must be vacated immediately.

Send the boss a sure-fire, get-rich-quick stock pick that's guaranteed to lose.

Hire the city's most expensive decorator to redo the boss's office while the boss is out of town.

◆

Sign up the boss for every major charity golf tournament in town.

◆

Hide a carpenter ant farm in the boss's prized cherry wood desk.

◆

Call the boss at 3 a.m. and when the boss answers have the voice say, "Is it OK to talk now, honey?"

Obtain the boss's calling-card number and call every 900 dial-a-porn number you can find.

◆

When the boss is away, fill the house's basement with water from the garden hose creating an indoor swimming pool.

◆

Send a next-day delivery of a gross of edible underwear to the boss's office.

CONCLUSION

While we have suggested some light-hearted and in some cases downright dastardly ways of dealing with some difficult work-related situations created by a boss, we would like to close on a serious note. Not only may some problems bosses create be annoying, some may actually lead to your leaving your job at your initiative or your boss's. Should it appear that such a situation may be in the making, we suggest the following:

1. Keep a journal. Make notes to yourself that describe the situation on a daily basis. You may need to establish a pattern of repeated behaviors by your boss. This information could be valuable.

2. Always remain calm. Never, never let your boss put you in a situation where you lose control.

3. If it's not in writing, it hasn't happened. Document everything. Communicate in writing with your boss as much as possible. Follow verbal conversations with something in writing expressing your understanding of the exchange. Keep copies, preferably not at work. Wherever possible, make sure that others have copies so that someone other than your boss is aware of what you are doing.

4. Take a stand; especially when others are present. Don't let the boss walk all over you. State your position and your reasons for it. If your boss doesn't want to listen, your co-workers will get the message about who is creating the problem.

5. Be careful of the people with whom you share your problems. Loyalties may shift (or even evaporate) once you are viewed as being "on the outside, looking in."

6. Realize that you probably won't change your boss's personality. Be prepared to consider leaving your position. Before doing so, consider all of the options. Some ways to leave are better than others in terms of immediate compensation and long-term career considerations.

7. If it looks like things are really heating up, seek legal advice. If you have done some of the things mentioned already, you will be in a better position when you consult an attorney. Remember, some things bosses do go beyond being annoying or even prerogatives of the office; they may be illegal. Some of the areas most commonly involved include age and sex discrimination, sexual harassment, constructive discharge, slander and defamation of character. Your attorney can help you understand the legal definition of these terms and assist you in selecting your options.

8. Don't isolate yourself. Seek out family and trusted friends who can provide a refuge and an opportunity to focus on matters not related to work.

9. Don't withdraw from the responsibilities of your position. Continue to meet and attempt to exceed your job responsibilities.

10. Whatever the situation, remember that a job is a means to more important ends. No job is worth dreading the thought of going to work each day. Don't wait until everything you have worked for, especially your personal and family life, suffers. Do something positive about it.

Readers are encouraged to send us their own "Get Evens" or interesting office anecdotes. All submissions become the property of the authors but if we print yours, we'll give you credit for it — unless you tell us that you want to remain anonymous. Send them to Barbara and Roger Sorochty at the following address:

4275 34th St., S. #153
St. Petersburg, FL 33711

Video Poker Mania, by Dwight & Louise Crevelt, $4.95. A hot new sequel to the authors' bestselling *Slot Machine Mania,* based on the authors' beliefs that most players are being duped into playing the wrong strategies to win.

Co-author Dwight Crevelt is a veteran designer and engineer of today's high-tech slot machines, and the only author to have written on this subject from inside the slot industry.

As proof of their contention, the authors cite internal information that confirms a glaring fact that few players know: *Video poker machines are holding a much larger percentage of profit for the casinos than they're supposed to!*

Their discovery has led them to devise a set of *three* new strategies, based on different types of players and different methods of play. They no longer believe that one strategy is right for everyone. Find out which new strategy is right for you!

Slot Machine Mania, by Dwight & Louise Crevelt, $4.95. Slot machines are the fastest growing segment of the casino and sure to get bigger. It's been estimated that over 30 million people in the U.S. are frequent players. *Slot Machine Mania* is perfect for these players as the most comprehensive, up-to-date volume on slots and video poker!

Virtually everything is covered: how to judge percentages and select more favorable machines; money management; common misconceptions; superstitions; cheating methods and regulations; casino promotions; and million-dollar jackpot winners.

Beat The Track, by Ada Kulleck, $4.95. *Beat The Track* stands out among the hodge-podge of horse-racing books now on the market. Covering both thoroughbred-racing and harness-racing, the author writes from the heart to give the reader a sincere and realistic understanding of what it's like to bet and handicap horses.

Carefully structured for both the novice and serious player, the author details her two-decade success at Southern California tracks, from how to read the Daily Racing Form, to how to eliminate losers. Her logical, sensible, easy-to-learn methods have fooled the most respected handicappers.

Lifestyles Of A High Roller, by Phyllis Wolff, $5.95. Experience what it's like to be treated like royalty; to have the casino cater to your every need. From lavish suites to limo service; from ringside seats at all the shows to gourmet dining every evening... you'll meet celebrities, attend VIP parties, and enjoy high-stakes action in the casino.

As the wife of one of the casino's most sought-after high rollers, the author presents a diary account of their many exciting trips to Las Vegas, Atlantic City, the Bahamas... wherever the action is non-stop, and the treatment is fit for a king.

Off The Strip, by Moe Shuckelman and Mark Lewis, $4.95. A collection of gambling jokes and cartoons that makes for a truly unique book. You'll laugh at these great cartoons by Mark Lewis who covers just about everything from video poker to swim-up blackjack tables. And Moe Shuckelman's jokes poke fun at just about everyone, from pit bosses to sore losers. *Off The Strip* is a refreshing break from the serious side of the games. Makes a great gift!

Las Vegas & Reno Area Fun Guide, by Derotha Sourwine, $3.95. Written by a born-and-raised Nevada writer, the FUN GUIDE's "inside" advantage really comes through in the many personal tips to the reader that only a "local" could offer. Her "very readable" style is a refreshing change of pace from the typical travel guide or simple directory.

In addition, the reader will truly enjoy the author's expression of Nevada's natural scenic beauty from the intriguing desert to the High Sierras... from Lake Mead to Lake Tahoe... from nearby Death Valley to the Grand Canyon.

Special attention is given to attractions the entire family — especially the kids — will enjoy, from theme parks to the famous Ponderosa Ranch.

Casino Games, by John Gollehon, $5.95. The only mass-market paperback that covers *all* the games: blackjack, craps, roulette, baccarat, keno, video poker, slot machines, and sports betting!

Casino Games differs vastly from all the other "how to play" books because simply knowing "how to play" isn't enough. What makes this book a strong seller is the author's critical commentary on discipline, money management, and common sense; how to recognize an opportunity that most players never see.

Gollehon teaches the reader *how to win!*

The Book Of Famous Places, by Diane Burton Robb, $5.95. Perhaps the most unique travel book on the market, *The Book Of Famous Places* is a travel guide, history book, and reference book to our nation's historic sites.

Divided into three sections: Wars, Discovery, and Presidents, this fascinating book covers our history in a most readable way, providing rare insight into historically famous personalities and little known facets of history-making events. Sure to be a hit with trivia fans too!

Gollehon books are available at many of the leading national-chain bookstores and at hotel and airport newsstands. The publisher regrets it cannot fulfill orders directly from the consumer except for quantity orders (contact: Special Sales). If a book is unavailable at your favorite bookstore, tell them to order it through Ingrams for prompt delivery usually within 48 hours.

Prices, availability, and book specifications subject to change without notice.